War in the Genes

and other poems

War in the Genes

and other poems

Poems by Ralph Salisbury

Cherry Grove Collections

Published by Cherry Grove Collections
P.O. Box 541106
Cincinnati, OH 45254-1106

Typeset in Baskerville by WordTech Communications LLC,
Cincinnati, OH

ISBN: 1932339701
LCCN: 2004108513

Poetry Editor: Kevin Walzer
Business Editor: Lori Jareo

Visit us on the web at www.cherry-grove.com

Acknowledgments

This is to gratefully acknowledge that some of these poems were first published in the following journals and anthologies.

Journals:

Anthropology and Humanism
Bellingham Review
The Colorado Quarterly
Massachusetts Review
New Letters
North Carolina Quarterly
Northwest Review
The Pacific
Periphery
Perspective
Prism International
Silverfish Review
The Southern Oregon Currents
West Coast Review

Anthologies:

Circle of Motion
Men Talk
The Smith: America II
Songs from this Earth on Turtle's Back
This Should Be Enough
Warnings, an Anthology on the Nuclear Peril

This book is dedicated to Ingrid Wendt,
my wife of 37 years,
splendid poet and worker and defender of the human race.

Contents

I. Conquistadores, Conquered and Continent: Some Colonial Histories

A Coastal Temple Ruin, 1992 15
Montezuma's Castle—Cliff Dwelling—Arizona 16
The U.S. Bombs a Hospital for the Mentally Ill While Invading Grenada,
    Which Spain Originally Took from Indians.................. 17
Potato-Planting, a Native History 18
War in the Genes, a Reveille for Mustering the Dead 19
The Five-Hundred Year War 20
An Historian Kills Time while Awaiting a Pre-Dawn Train-Subway
    Connection................... 21
The Little Match Girl—and Boy 23
Black Smoke 24
A Carpenter's Native American History 25
Murder in a Cathedral, Investigation 2003 26
Jesus Among the Yunwiya, and a Second Coming 27
Space Probe 28

II. A Natural History of a Struggle with, and a Love of, Nature

Banking a Farmhouse 33
Wood Stacked but Left to Rot, New England, 1992 35
Cherokee Manhood-Vigil Vision 36
For A Killer 37
A Soldier, Hunter and Father's Gratitude Words 38
Three For My Pacifist Son, Brian 39
Medicine-Meeting, Hoopa, 1994 40
A Benign Selfishness 41
Wild Goose, Eaten, and Owl, Knitted to Hang on Wall 42
A Ritual Seeking a Voice 43

III. An Unnatural History, the Killing of One's Own Kind

The Battle of the Bulge 47
Konstanz, Germany, 1992, Columbus Year 48
Castration of the Herd-Boar Recollected without Tranquility after
    Nagasaki 49
From the Back of the Refrigerator 51
A Two-Band Rainbow: In Memory of Corporal "X" 52
His Country Intending "Regime Change" in Another Country, He Takes a
    Walk, Good, He Is Told, for His Aging Constitution 53
Before 9/11/01, and After 54

The Gulf: Another, Lost, Indian War... 56

IV. An History of a War Against Time
A Natural Perspective 59
Elephant Shoes 60
Slitting the Tongue, So That Crow Should Be Parrot 62
Window, Squirrel, Cat 63
A Hunt for Food 65
A Cherokee Ars Poetica.. 66
Two in Memory of E.L. Mayo... 67
We Knew Them 69
In the Air Of.. 70
A View of El Greco's Toledo 72
Snow Geese, Literary Suppression, and Benito Mussolini 73
Out of This World 74
An Indian War, Possibly Not the Last... 76

V. An History of a Struggle For and Against Love
Between Skeletal Trees.. 79
A High School Student's Guide to World War Two 80
Glowing Flakes Flicked 81
For a Peace Corps Worker.. 82
The Fat Spanish Fisherwoman, Red-Sweatered,................................. 83
Ascending a Madrone Tree for a View of the Pacific, and Remembering
    the Columbus Day Storm... 84
Love Poem for a Woman Who Is a Complete Stranger........................ 85
Sunrise Incident on Train, Starting to Start Over............................... 86
Storm, Atlantic and Pacific 87

VI. An History of Some Struggles Against Extinction
The Beautiful Silver.. 91
To Win Love 92
Snowbound in Deep Woods 93
Knitting Needles Warm.. 94
For Martina Erin Marie, My Newborn Daughter................................ 95
Driving from My Daughter's Birth... 96
Girl Passing House Where I Live with Wife and Baby Daughter........... 97
Aeons of Wishes 98
New Oil into Old Leather...100
A Widower, the Old Geologist Tries Not to Awake 101
Sunset and Lilacs 102
History or Some...103
Veterans Day, 2002, Politicians Threatening War 104

VII. A Vanishing American's Struggle Against Vanishing

A Ritual to Not Feel Alone 107
For My Swinomish Brother Drumming Across the Water...................108
Sleep Chant..109
Age 77, I Climb to Indian Ridge's Fire-Lookout Tower and Search for
    Lineage 110
After Heart Surgery..111
After Heart-Bypass Surgery, Another Ritual for Continuing Struggle...112
Caring for the Soon to be Born 113
A Prophecy, Wish, Hope or Prayer 114

I. Conquistadores, Conquered and Continent: Some Colonial Histories

A Coastal Temple Ruin, 1992

For Octavio Paz and Cesar Vallejo

Surf echoing Spanish cannon, or Aztec drums
summoning centuries of slain,
victory-regalia-petals proclaim sun
ascendant, while rainbows wing
from nests, to split banana beaks and sing
aeons-extinct sea-verge-ecology ancestries,
clouds, roots, fragrance, fruit
offering survivors of war in the genes more
than invaders took
and defenders gave
their lives trying to save.

Montezuma's Castle—Cliff Dwelling—Arizona

"Sivapu," hole in the earth, from which people first issued into being.
—Myth of the Hopi and others.

For their "population-explosion"—when
the Pinta, Nina and Santa Maria were
two hundred years from any shore—
the Sinagua built high-rise apartments,
whole trees propped root-end up
to support defense-minded generations' weight.

Horizon dust sighted from sentinel loft—"Invasion"—

or "Drought," only wind flowing through irrigation-gates,
yearning lovers' starving seed
shriveling in the womb—

the Sinagua fled

into scholars' guesses, passed on to
an Indian survivor,
surrounded by Sivapu-deep
nuclear missile wells.

The U.S. Bombs a Hospital for the Mentally Ill While Invading Grenada, Which Spain Originally Took from Indians

Pilots, assigned
to take care of the sound of mind
administered shock treatments to the insane,
and planes, like gulls, their nesting done,
were lighter returning to sea,

from which, like out-
of-season hurricanes,
Manifest Destiny's weaponry came,
for centuries.

It came again —
as incendiary angels descended, not
from cathedrals' carved heights
but from the U.S.A.,

imposing military history
on natives already as civilized
and Christianized as
explosions and sperm could make them,
Indian genes islands, invaders' blood
flooding my veins and Earth.

Potato-Planting, a Native History

"The duty of the writer in violent times is to keep history alive."
Laura Restrepo, Colombian novelist

Our knives honed thin
as spring's last edge
of ice, we peel brown skins
thick so sprouts will root

and we can eat summer
through winter,
as generations did, before

conquerors skinned men,
seeking to find gold they thought
to be hidden in mines—and, now,
in supermarket-bins, they put
potatoes, wet not to rot
till sold,

by whites,
to whites,

where Indians planted Indians
in Indians in Indian land.

War in the Genes, a Reveille for Mustering the Dead

Once what someone once called Keats,
"a stable-boy," brisk brushing startling blood into flood,
under my hair, as white
as clouds grandchildrens' nuclear bombers comb, I write
of grooming descendants of battle-steeds
abandoned by Spaniards to free
galleons' holds for New World gold, and, war,
for Arab oil, now on, ink colts
of colts of chargers and get
of get of soldiers are risen, again,
in mind, as is Indian blood, in scalp,
as is sun, this day, of my few or fewer, begun.

The Five-Hundred Year War

for a sister in battle

Her husband's too proud to take government aid
and won't join his work-mates on strike.
A storm-window-maker, but what
does he know of tornado, I
and my family, huddled in cellar, survived.

The English he's born from took Spaniards' "Chalaque,"
taken from "Tsaragi"— Choctaw for "cave-men"—
"Cherokee," now, trade-name for cars,
even our slave name enslaved.

His wife—religious, courageous, the swell
of her belly mortality, beauty—marches for
ending imperialism's Five-Hundred Year War,

which threatens her children
and everyone's,

scars, in my body and brain,
petals, for her and for all like her.

An Historian Kills Time while Awaiting a Pre-Dawn Train-Subway Connection

for Florence Howe, Judy Chicago, Faith Frost, Ingrid Wendt,
and other leaders in today's struggle for equality

Where neon paints fertility-rite allure
and buttons shine like dimes in nylon's wish-
ing-pool-rippling over tip-engendering promises of
mammalian love, he nurses warm tea, secure
from dangers native to blackness backing glass,
the only hint of the Enlightenment
his pale reflection reflecting on
Manifest Destiny's history.

    In the tradition of the Phoenicians
    selling shellfish to tint royal robes
    and harems' skimpy silk,
    entrepreneurial Indians load furs
    on steeds, abandoned by Spaniards,
    who'd found their rumored gold
    was copper—shapable into slave girls' rings
    and trade-trail bells,
    to summon neighboring warriors as customers,
    "That copper now forged for
    Emancipator-portrait coins,"
    ghost servers sneer, their breast-
    bones bare, in imagination, where—
    the thin-as-air-of-prayers libations quaffed—
    dead conquerors leave
    memories as gratuities, all free,
    presumably, for eternity.

Time killed by rumination,
Time's analyst's interred,
as scheduled, under slums,

and, as his time-table prophesied,
he rises among
billboard profusions of mercantile confusions,
young women offering the world,
in offering white skin,
and teeth, to a risen,
and soon-to-be-waning, sun.

The Little Match Girl—and Boy

*for my brother Leland, who died from malnutrition
and illness in his first year*

His stone, smaller than dictionary, same size
as storybook, my brother did not live to read,

between some grown Christian writer's lines,

how cold a child had been,

her never-to-be-desired,
never-to-be-motherly body bearing matches,
to sell for shelter and food,

small flames illuminating faces, which anticipate
the pleasures of expensive cigars—

and illuminating, blindingly, sunlit sky
over children, born, unborn and never to be born,
in inconceivable,
parasol-twirling, dragon-kite-flying, Japan.

Black Smoke

(i)

My brother starving and ill and gone,
Before his first wish—

Dad hunting, from dawn
Until unable to aim, to keep
Surviving children alive—

I'd draw forts, as round
As birthday-cakes,
And arrows like candles ablaze,

On grocery-mailers' frost sides,

Whose sun—a politician's post-mark-clouded portrait—shone
Above address-name,
Our family's official designation,
In tombstone-rows
Since England's invasion.

(ii)

As black as the ink of one Cherokee history,
Dollar-signs curled like smoke,
From unaffordable cakes.

They curl again,
Rice burned and families turned
Into candles, in
An Asian nation,
Someone's wish come true, not mine.

A Carpenter's Native American History

*"American history is false, for the most part,
because American historians find more success
in presenting a positive view."*

*American historian,
lecturing in Germany,
1992*

Battered red by factory steel,
this trigger-finger nail's
a tv-movie-brave's face,

its lower curve the white
of enamel, gritted, while

pale people ink,
in hospital numerals,

one Native American history—
of injury, unemployability
and family hunger—
as indifferently as if—

Egyptian tombs and Roman catacombs
gold-mines on American screens—

others' last chapters could
not ever be theirs.

Murder in a Cathedral, Investigation 2003

(1)

Removed from the skull of one earl,
"exhumed and re-interred in the new cathedral,"
this rat is exhibit A, displayed
beside Stone Age Stonehenge weaponry—
to prove that "the Lord had been poisoned."

(2)

Similarly, "Polar bear meat infested with trichinae,"
discovered in the innards of explorers dug
from decades of frozen snow,
it is thought that ship's garbage's uncooked pork
drifted as ice, possibly for centuries before
a brother carnivore's mouth melted a taste
not native to any sea.

(3)

An unsuspecting, uninvited and late dinner-guest,
the rat, too, found something new in what had been thought just meat,
and our investigation of an Age of Kings crime's
implications for our own and future times should add
that another noble victim died in the Crusades.

Oil-barrels our generation's Holy Grails,
the "tallest of all Europe's spires,"
Peter the Rock's brandished stone spear
inscribes, on the heavens, reminder of
a nuclear-rocket near here.

Jesus Among the Yunwiya, and a Second Coming

He was, they say, like Chief Guwisguwi, faithful, as were white ministers, imprisoned because they would not betray their Indian parishioners—Christ faithful, though nails spread arms, like wings of a dove.

They say he'd been tested, beaten and crowned, thorns turned to turn all bloody the head they surrounded, not like antlers turned to battle a rival, not like Spain's and England's chieftains' crown-prongs thrust into the heavens and carved upon weapons bloodying so easily they conquered no one though defeating everyone. For generations, worth was numbers of breaths drawn before pain broke brave down to beast. Jesus drew many breaths.

They say he has risen, but—though shafts remain in hands—arrowheads strike the children of children unborn, wings those of a Raven Mocker witch, plunging to eat our hearts, our years, unlived, prolonging, they say forever, the life of one who first came armed only with words of love.

"Yunwiya" (which can be translated as "we the people") is the name those of us now called "Cherokee" called ourselves, before invasion by Spaniards, whose Spanishization of the Choctaw insult word "Tsaragi" (approximateable as "cave-dwellers") was something like "Chalaque," later Anglicized as "Churakee" and Americanized as "Cherokee" (the name a U.S. auto company took for a vehicle, which my family might be able to afford if our ancestors' 2000-acre plantation had not been expropriated, by right of "Manifest Destiny," in the Southeast, as, later, many more acres, with oil under, would be expropriated in Oklahoma—as, later, property of Jews would be expropriated in Hitler's Germany).

Information, though not the sentence-length, from James Mooney, from my father and from others.

Space Probe

Not the spaceship gleaming over lunar craters, as black
as the plowing I'd done since dawn, & not the neat little gun
with which I could have zapped everybody bigger than me
& not even the girl, whose tight-flight-suited waist
I could clasp & the spurts of my rocket would move us
to where not even the imagination had ever been—

not these but the Indian mound,
around which not only I
but my older brothers, father & grandfather had had to plow—
heart-high-grass jade sacrifice-blades,
bull-thistles' head-tall purple blossoms royal jewels set
in sword-pronged crowns; sunflowers brown
against frost—& never an arrow-chip, let alone
a tomahawk-cleft bone, to prove
what generations had believed—

belief preserving an island, green
in plowing's gleaming black sea,
an island succoring seed
for whose blooms there were no names,
the country around, in anyone's memory.

That island in my mind, in a world
surrounded by darkness untouched by a sun, said
to be slowly turning cold—
that island in my mind,
in a world which is always
turning to something supposedly new—
that island is, presumably, also turning, but
it *is*—it simply *is*, & it is to it I'd turn—the pages
of comic-strip spaceships burned,
or turned brown in the basement,
& even the headlines
HIROSHIMA ATOM-BOMBED less black
as paper decomposes in the files.

It is to that island that I try
to turn, as, around the bones
of an Indian slave—who became a king,
dethroned by awakening—
the flesh of a man, who'd be, simply, free, grows
too old for war or for cavorting with an astronaut girl
over Old Glory drooping in airless craters of what once was,
in times perhaps more simple, simply a heavenly body or
a poetic symbol for love.

II. A Natural History of a Struggle with, and a Love of, Nature

Banking a Farmhouse

in memory of Aunt Jennie, my other mother

Before winter is worse and wind is the screech of a witch
plunged out of clouds, to eat our hearts and take

the years we'd have lived, we stake,
around our foundation, woven wire,

which held rambunctious rams,
and corral, into insulating wall,

straw, too imbued with manure
to serve any longer as animal bedding.

Not like schoolbooks' dikes
raised against sea,

ours helps boards hold heat
flooded from burned stove-wood,

helps cloth to hold warmth
released from flesh,

and we survive the months
when snowflakes seed earth,

accumulating, then, like grain in bins, into mounds
as high as ones raised

to aid a centuries-dead tribes'
memory of loved ones gone.

Our foundation's banking, our salvation, plowed
to feed crops, in the benign season, I'd stake,
around everyone's common home,

the air we share, woven into words,
to fence sufficient summer

against what's as certain as

our worst intentions to kill
us all, in time.

Wood Stacked but Left to Rot, New England, 1992

Unlike some, too evil or too inconsequential to tell,
this history's of oxidation's returning to earth
sustained by aeons of suns, a tree,
whose ancestors shaded Vanishing Americans.

Its wood, like the sweat of whoever chopped
and stacked it, will vanish without having warmed
any destinies trekking in human genes
or having been even one chapter in
Extinction by Ozone-Destruction.

What's next will be
told by the wind, but, still,
betrothals' and condolences' roses' glows
may light the way home for more
centuries of beauty than any history can say.

Cherokee Manhood-Vigil Vision

Among stones enormous as buffalo,
a beast fiercer than panther
and knowing the intricacies
of vines, brambles and trees,
is maybe a bear, fur black like your hair,
teeth as white as your
grave-spade-shape Indian incisors, and

you must learn to climb, batter, claw, bite, meat raw
on your tongue ever after until, already meat,
yourself, you can dream you are more.

For A Killer

"It is the blight that man was born for,
It is Margaret you mourn for."

"Spring and Fall, to a Young Child"
Father Gerard Manley Hopkins

Caucasian and civilized,
she hated hunting's having provided food for
her Indian neighbor—from 12,
until, 18, he learned
to butcher her army's way—but,

the refrigerator door
slammed on her daughter's kitten, she called for
a killer to kill her child's pretend child,
for mercy, and mourned the death
of the civilization Columbus' invasion had become
for her little girl's little girl mom.

A Soldier, Hunter and Father's Gratitude Words

for my son Jeff
and for deer we and our people before us hunted

Since words could feed
generations beyond my generation's last hunger, I hunt,
again, on a glacier a lifetime of suns must thaw
before prints of deer I killed will disappear,

as will flesh venison fed, and fear
of inching over frozen rain,
feeling at one with those
exploring the heavens' cold
unknown, and with artists trying not to die
from Time's snowstorm erasures, bone hand's brush-
strokes kindling fire generous enough to warm the world,

and to cook, for children's children, centuries of browse's

lineage, in cells of an animal, whose fleeing hoofs—
like the tongues of forebear poets—abraded a trail
through ice and saved my life.

Three For My Pacifist Son, Brian

on his 29th birthday, 14 July, Bastille Day,
1982, 490th year of a war for survival

I

Last century's bones unable to fill
bellies, or minds, our deer and words
become history, my dad
had only money enough to buy—
from ice on a truck, moving, as slow
as a silver glacier—buffalo, squaw-fish,
or suckers, although a waiting-room's *Field*
and Stream's Cutthroat Trout lunkers had gleamed
like bumpers of the loan-shark banker's new car.

II

When the Mississippi—crossed by Cherokees
mid-winter on The Trail of Tears—thawed,

sheepshead, pickerel, pike, blue-gills and gar
grazed in our cattle-pasture, and Teacher quipped that
the Ordovician'd returned, but I wrote fish'n.

III

Then, when neighbors' ancestors' Thor or
our Thunderer's *blitzkrieg* battalions of rain invaded roads,
sixteen and innocently ready to go to war
in an army which had killed millions, for gold
and land, I'd wade to read history's praise
of "Civilized Man's Manifest Destiny,"
my toenails compass needles, I follow, three—
like the Christian trinity—wars later, to try
to learn what minnows seem born knowing, the way.

Medicine-Meeting, Hoopa, 1994

for my compassionate sister Ruth

Telling the gathering I'm Cherokee—

  my skin, like the skins
  of many of them, the skin
  of soldiers who tore
  futures not rightfully theirs
  from the genes of defeated populations—

my answers are Father's mother's: "Sassafras tea
for congested lungs; mint leaves
for troubled digestion; willow bark chewed
for pain; tobacco breathed,
into aching ears"—

  and words of love,
  to raise the dead

  in children's dreams
  of living as women and men.

A Benign Selfishness

in memory of my brother Leland

A hummingbird, small
as an out-of-season grape
on a pine's crucifix-shape top,

my body smaller, if seen at all
by bombardier or God, I warm,

each hour, a plastic flower's red-
as-communion-wine ice, to save,

while millions of children are starving still,
these years after my little brother's last hunger,

one tiny migrant, which weakness or faith
keeps resident,

what it might be to be
a merciful angel more
than I can hope to feel.

Wild Goose, Eaten, and Owl, Knitted to Hang on Wall

for my mother, Olive Ione McAllister

Gray petal, soon to fall from crimson dawn,
a wild goose, hearing me imitate a call
to join a gaggle of strangers for dinner is met
by flocks of shot,

and life, which flew thousands of miles
through air, shared with words, stills
between teeth, retriever, resolute
as poet, struggling against
the current to bring the dead
back to the living's need.

No phoenix flight of trilling syllables,
my feeding-call's honks lured meat
for Mother to cook, for our family to eat.

Her fingers, as ceaseless as wings
seeking sufficient summer, wove red yarn
into the blossoms on a bough an owl's black
prey-piercing claws above me clutch, while,
stark winter years to endure, I try
to make my pen knit
another migrant's flight,

warm Gulf, ancestors' nesting place,
a future to hope for, though far.

A Ritual Seeking a Voice

Though the bedroom where I was born's become
one end of the living room, three—
like the Trinity Mother was buried believing in—walls,
of the space where I protested the world's first blow—
from a doctor's well-intentioned hand—still stand.

The fourth—four sacred to Cherokees, including me—
the fourth, which hid all but the sounds of birth, is gone.

Bed-rung a limb ancestors, conceived by Darwin, knew
as perch—I perched and saw the baby I'd been,
eyes shut against frightening light,
my brother's cries, and mine, and everyone's,
soon doomed to summon from a room,
without a door, a voice, and hands, and breast
to help us to dream peacefully.

III. An Unnatural History, the Killing of One's Own Kind

The Battle of the Bulge

for my brother Bob, combat veteran WWII

Creating, on rations envied by nations at peace,
girths of a size befitting citizens
of "The Greatest Nation on Earth,"
an atom-bomb-armed population called their surrender
to knives and forks and spoons
"The Battle of the Bulge,"
taking in vain the name of the victory,
in which sons lost all of the weight they'd had.

Looking at books boys carried to hide groins'
intentions, girls giggled, "The Battle of the Bulge,"
each nuclear-age future mother able to dream
her belly a mound
blessed by a cross.

Konstanz, Germany, 1992, Columbus Year

for Martin Christadler, a scholar of our time

Konstanz's fooling a religious rival, by
inviting then burning him, recalls Spain's,
Holland's and England's treachery
in treaties, which hid intentions of genocide,
when they invaded Native American land,

and, in the 20th Century,
this city's deluding bombardiers, by
leaving its lights burning, like those
of its Swiss neighbor, recalls
a German friend—only a boy, then—
bicycling warning, through other cities' unlit streets,
that Americans were flying to burn
women and children and men,
who could only try to hide in the dark.

Sun blazing in stained-glass wings,
the millions martyred by incineration, take flight,
and cathedral stones avalanche ashen shade
· onto a man whose bombs dropped, and drop,
their shadows somewhere
other than here.

Castration of the Herd-Boar Recollected without Tranquility after Nagasaki

in memory of my brother Ray

Manila's fibers conquered by Japan,
and the Mayan Peninsula's sisal-rope
tripping a body bigger than Dad's,

our herd-boar struck earth, a three-hundred pound bomb's
explosions of dust becoming mud on my tongue,

as I helped to hold down generations of tons
enraged that they would not ever be born,

my father's knife reducing their sire's
answers for sows' desires to
the lowest common denominator,
plant-fertilizer, the remainder shoat-meat,
removal of testicles having made dinners
sweeter for genteel tables.

My shy, highflying dream—

of being a military hero,
for movie-beauty impossibly above me—

became a damaged plane,
seeking, in vain, a place to land,

a bomber pilot's brain
a crucial engine strained
by one mission too many—

as chopsticks dropped

into a plateful of shattered glass,
shards hari-kari blades
for enemy foetal cells.

From the Back of the Refrigerator

The mold that jelly grows,
a gray bracelet of fur
surrounding bloody marrow;

the fear that the groin will crumble, that
the heart, like a breakfast egg,
will shatter on kitchen gleams; that

the boss's test-tube eyes
will one day turn slightly cloudy; that

a Red Chinese, blue cuff
braceleting tense fingers,
will trace red veins on a map—

and that the final day.

A Two-Band Rainbow: In Memory of Corporal "X"

Promoted, two stripes, for so
    many enemies—for only one
    of our own, a fence will fend him, from me,
    from you, till words forge barbs into bars
    berserk flesh can bludgeon itself against
    without harming even the tiniest particle
    of steel—and forge, then, rifles for
    a firing squad's fusillade.

The years not
    army enough to still
    tongue wriggling through "Eden's" dust between
    uncoiled barbed strands' sharp fangs,
    he lives again,
    "Cherokee," like me,
    but "Christian...Cain"—his "Abel"
    his rival, white,
    the beautiful—the terrified-
    into-willingness—woman Asian, as were men reborn,
    as two-stripe-rainbow
    adorning uniform,

    his story ours—

    who did as he did
    or nothing—

    the ending: calendar numbers on stone,
    sum one minus one.

His Country Intending "Regime Change" in Another Country, He Takes a Walk, Good, He Is Told, for His Aging Constitution

You find on the road   dropped
from a car   that crashed
thigh-fondling miles further on
or only had to be towed   a bolt
worn spiral of its threads
gleaming in sun   a silver circular-stair
to heaven   just junk you pick up
to use   or to keep nature pure   or don't

the president intent
on his speech   the crowd
around so favorably or angrily loud
neither he nor his body-guards hear
an inconsequential click
like that of a voting-machine
the war   intended   or unforeseen
averted   or started   and
for everyone in it   lost
whatever history may say   and   yes,
in battles   observers observe
most bullets merely fall.

Before 9/11/01, and After

for my daughter, Martina

Oregon coastal cannon could not still
One from a submarine, and a Sunday school class
Was sent to heaven because we
Machine-gunners, training to kill
Others, who'd try to down our bombers, had failed to see
A Japanese balloon, as it had descended, bearing bombs
Intended to burn acres and acres of
Billions of dollars worth of centuries of trees,
Whose great-grandparents were not even cones when
A galleon, hold empty for gold, sailed
Further offshore than any spear could reach
And cannonaded villages,
Which might have resisted invasion.

As steadfast as those sacrificing lives
To their conception of God, my countrymen
Are offering what syllables as beautiful as petals,
Wilting, have always said, and,
Recalling Nazi firing squads'
Eliminating future sabotage, I take
No satisfaction from Afghanistan's or
Iraq's destruction. Instead, I hear the dead,
Whose deaths I and millions of my generation intended,
Their homes, blown into tombs, become
The sorrowing tones of a friend,
The conquerors'—*our*—language now his.

At 17, a volunteer, at 25, a resister, I lived
By the words of orators.
At 75, survivor of a heart attack
And cancer, I heed the silence of thousands in
My daughter's voice,
Phoning, three miles from explosions, to reassure

Her mother and me
Just after the World Trade Center went down.

The Gulf: Another, Lost, Indian War

for my grandsons, Travis and Connor

Yesterday's snow
on black bark in Iraq,
an Indian—in
the army which took
his ancestors' land, for gold and furs and slaves,
and now takes Arabs' oil—

dreams forests felled to build
the Byzantine Empire's navy's tyranny brief as the heat
of a bullet, that left no king
to exact revenge

on humans, as numerous as flakes
which make yesterday's charred
history of battle as inconceivable
as words that soon
must be written to next of kin.

IV. An History of a War Against Time

A Natural Perspective

Pale contrails bandaging sky,
warplanes sound
imitations of victims' screams,

and, in a bomber no longer, I am
a needle Mom wove "Home
Sweet Home" with or patched the pants
of a poet-to-be
she'd hoped
would study and doctor and keep alive
some small as himself
for a time.

Elephant Shoes

in memory of Earle Birney

A good fight inviting as a good road
invites, a man, knuckles beginning to tingle, may,
like his country, try
a little travel, but I
remember army armored cars
scattered, like meteors torn off stars.

Love? Traditional poetry's rose-petals tent, pitched,
ditched and staked against storm, bare beauty swims
science's lava up mountain, eager to be mine,
in my mind, but,
on reaching snow-quilted summit, dives
to center the earth, and, I—a far from ideal
idealizing man—I

abide in a rented house, work 40 hours a week,
for someone I dislike, like many of you, and picnic in
our public wishes, resenting your noise, as you do mine,
but, when you shamble over to offer the use
of the fire you have made for hot-dogs or one
of those obscure metaphors about weather
nobody ever understands, I feel like crying
so long our kids would have a salt lake, to sail
news-print ships—The HIROSHIMA, The NAGASAKI—half
across, and, if I do not cry, not daring to risk
melting the ice all of us skate
toward eventual summer, forgive me for being
no better than you,
a poet who will stumble and fall
over a final syllable,
though living for good moments, which sometimes seem oftener
and longer, sometimes not. Forgive me
this early morning verse

sputtering like a power mower almost out of gas
below your bedroom window, when you
were maybe in the best dream of your whole life
so far or loving your wife
or feeling your own poem
scampering into its den
ahead of the alarm clock's steel-edged bicuspids and
the god-awful elephant shoes
of the usual things that you have to do.

Slitting the Tongue, So That Crow Should Be Parrot

Let's say—

for our ears are carved to hear—

when there are
no roars, explosions, screams—

memory's mumble—

let's say that I caught a crow,
whose wing would no longer take air
and would take weeks to forget Dad's bullet.

Let's say, that I slit a tongue
as stiff as a quill I'd halved into reed
and, with my breath,
made "Yankee Doodle" clear
enough for parents, teacher and, even big kids
to guess. Or say what I'd been told
was wrong, or I'd cut too deep, or, timid, too short
or couldn't cut at all,
and the cawing was only my own pain,
blade slipping, or plane,
intended to hurt Japanese, splitting air
a last time, earth
telling my bones
more than enlistment posters had.

Or say, our enemies customers again,
age bends my trigger-finger on pen,
and other suffering tongues must sing.

Window, Squirrel, Cat

for Henry James and Wallace Stevens

Except for this glass,
melted from sand—

whose molecules a man can de-
stabilize into syl-
lables—

except for this transparency—as clear as
my breath formed into words—in a real wall
cut from the dark
beneath bark—

and except for the aeons of processes and for
the generations preceding
an Irish war-widow of a German-American's marrying a Cherokee
and forming centuries
of possibilities—

except for all of the above,
this pen wouldn't be turning, into black ink, a black cat
stalking what can't be caught
and assimilated into feline cells

but what can be—
through my window's invisibility—
seen:

a squirrel, curled
like a question-mark, from tail
to a nose as round as a dot,
pressed to solidity seemingly visually
no more a barrier than air
of poetry or growls or squeals—

nostrils unable to catch the scent
of appetite apparently crouched to pounce,
through its own black fur,

which backs
the seeming nothing mirroring
a victim's invulnerable reflection.

A Hunt for Food

In forebears' words I have known long
enough to feel they are my own,
venison feeds flesh, become,
from many matings, mine,

and, bowstring's humming welcoming me
to a shared mortality, prey, not to be born,
print trails on centuries of trees' frosted leaves,
that children's children's children may be sustained
by whatever plants or animals die
to keep alive our own species, while sun
sustains everything that lives
on earth, on tongue.

A Cherokee Ars Poetica

Men blundering to make winter worse,
their war-clubs nuclear,

sycamores raise Cherokee forebears'
fingers in prayer, above
Grandfather River's obedience to long-

ago volcanoes' obedience to sun's flows'
obedience to laws no one living knows,

while aeons-extinct ancestral reptiles'
descendants erupt
as salmon-roe, each as round as our world, and

shooting-star smolts arc
splendor, through dark sea's sky,

which lovers' eyes,
mirrored and mirroring, may,
in wet black ink, say.

Two in Memory of E.L. Mayo

(1)

It is a formal decor, quite safe, you'd think,
if any place is, chair's tack-heads hippo-teeth,
their appetite lamplight, for bedtime-story and love.

A footstool plump as a hippo calf grins
a reminder of small friends
whose cap pistols captured your wigwam,
toppling poles blazing birthday candles you
wished on but not for a chair covered with the air
of words, tacked taut by stars. And who
wished what on them?

(2)

A gray sea of pipe-smoke's surges the tides
of Dad's worries, a white
life-preserver ring of light's afloat
among breakers of his own making,
and ballads, strummed and sung, become a poem,

in which, sinking, I grab the skeleton hand
of another father, a poet, who drowned in his own years
of cigarettes' assuagement of all
that verse cannot cure, and what he could not do
in life he does in book after book, swimming us ashore,
his parents in his mind,
their parents in theirs,
and on through time, his mother mine,
grief for Dad's death the owl
she wove, as I'd weave words,
black talons making more vivid the crimson blossoms she loved.

Pen, knitting-needle, owl-quill or thorn, for oar,
one woven petal's a bright

lifeboat loosed from its davits, to ply
gray sea to try
to keep ghosts afloat
in a ring of light.

We Knew Them

Nothing is
particular here. Red—not of
Indian skin
or roses—edges what could be
anyone's garden's
east and west and, then,
back into blackness again, and all
we care for,
a scar's pale summer-lightning on
a graceful knee
in a motel neoned like a hot-day-drink
in, maybe, Ohio—and bandaged,
when tiny, by somebody big—all moves,
like a vivid flock south—
or north—and

We knew them, we say,
knew names from a book between aardvark's
exploring nose and zoo's
zeroes shaped
like Columbus' propped eggs—

knew war-bonnet-feathers that flamed
and warmed us,
from scalp-locks' tousles to
chilblained,
wornout-moccasin-encumbered,
stubbed toes.

In the Air Of

We intersect here,
you plunging—by choice
or pushed—from
a skyscraper, and I

am working my way
up stairs, made

from words

or wood,

whose Indian name's gone,
like that of my tribe,
cut, as were forests, down,

railing ornate with brass's
imitation of New World gold,
glistening in sun,

which is falling, too.

You do not lack companionship.

We pass.

You ascend

the air of all
of the syllables
available,
for centuries, here,
in this conquered land
and raise sky-
scraper dynasties

from dictionaries
before
I have hit the street.

A View of El Greco's Toledo

Inside the bull-hide-tubful of offal, one sees,

on rags which wiped palette, sky
as blue as eyes turned toward gold

and sees bones
from a feast commemorating war
against Indian ancestors.

Then, in a world newer than The New,
older than The Old, one senses souls'

not giving a damn
for the skill artistic immortality demands,
winging their own bullheaded ways,

slain beast garmented again
in garbage-tub's stitched skin
and goring the satin matador's
shadow's agility
into an eternity
of savagery and beauty,

each person, mutt,
cat, bird, bat, fleeing, chasing, eating, mating and
snoring or soaring in his or her own way,

just as it should be,
naturally.

Snow Geese, Literary Suppression, and Benito Mussolini

While I am reading of advertisers' control over publishing,
a blizzard of birds gusts into orderly rows of commercially-grown
potatoes.

Honking insistently evidently sufficient traffic-control, I think:

Oh, Mussolini—whose decree forbade the din of auto horns—
how wrong you were. Your resurrection of Roman imperialism made
my older brother a prisoner of war, but, years after American victory,
Italian democracy's capital city's off-key symphony, in the state
    of Washington,
keeps bird-brained commuters from collisions of wings. Hear,
Old Freedom Suppressor—
though one generation and many million deaths too late—hear,
that this seemingly utterly disorderly cacophony, like poetry,
makes mating, makes nesting, makes a blizzard of birds,
beautiful in this dismal prelude to glorious spring—makes
everything worthwhile possible.

Out of This World

Many ways you could
choose to depart this nuclear-
aged-beyond-belief world,
but, grim too long,
you sneak out of camouflage-uniform
and into a real leaf's glowing corridors,
as if your utterly familiar,
though smaller, sticky feet
belonged no place
else—find everything

is upward-surging,

succumb,

evaporate off the tip
of the most recently formed bud

and are

as at home
in the air of
a fellow creature's saying
as ever

you were

in computer take-in, pay-out,
missile-launch file,

escaped
for good,
we could
idiomatically say,

your oldest forebears —
smelling of volcano—with you
all of the way.

An Indian War, Possibly Not the Last

for my brother Rex

A nuclear bomber—a silver crucifix
above ones made from gold—

A flying flicker—an arrowhead-shape,
red blaze on ashen nape
torching invaders' stockades—and

I fight an Indian war
again, not hand to hand,
but hand to pen,
taking a stab at
making less meaningless
a page's white skin,

To try to save a future for generations,

While losing my own,
and everyone's,
war against time.

V. An History of a Struggle For and Against Love

Between Skeletal Trees

Feathers, gray gusts of ash,
Igniting in sun,
Geese winging to Arctic to mate
And military jets blazing, above
Just-budded twigs, a man,
No longer a soldier, dreams
Of love's splendor, fledged
By his words to soar forever, though,
Inevitably to be as cold
As earth's breath thin around
A bomber—colder around
An ashen star.

A High School Student's Guide to World War Two

Our phantom candy/soft-drinks/beer
mingling with girls' gustatory ghosts
before parents' doors
shut, for a final time,

we shot, when commanded, at targets and hit

the children of
children's children's children, although

we had not aimed
ever to be other than lovers.

Glowing Flakes Flicked

Eaves rivers, stormed into gutters, then sea,
nests become rafts, I think of lineages meant
to share air with words
but doomed to fly
as fuel for flesh of fish,

whose fingerlings glitter like sparks,
spawned from harvesting-blades
and sharpening-wheel,
to disappear, as have
so many of my family,
into the dark, and I see stars,
which are similarly doomed,
our sun one of them,
impossibly beyond the furthest reach of mind,

as is a woman, her warmth gone
from memory, dream-children conceived
as light reflected off wheeling planets or off blade
honed for a harvest not destined to be made.

For a Peace Corps Worker

"When I saw you coming down that corridor, I almost cried,"
surprised a man who'd admired a girl's
courage in classroom battles, her love
of books and her desire
to help with the world's hunger.

Above his mouth, which had never lacked food,
or words of wisdom, his mustache a gray
horizon cloud this year, in a gaze as calm as pools
before a storm, he said that he himself
had sometimes felt like crying, coming down that corridor.

As shy as children they
would not again be
or have together, they
talked for a time
of timeless art
and did not question what they might have meant.

Hair, dark waves over depths he'd not ever sound,
eyes, ordinary stones ocean turns to sapphires in pitiless light,
and body, as slender as his wife's
before the babies, disappear
beyond the door, behind which he holds
his breath, to hear the final echoes of
a woman going to help with the world's hunger.

The Fat Spanish Fisherwoman, Red-Sweatered,

and scratching her ass, sways up the quay,
and geraniums sway, around concrete, which holds
the jostling sea from trawlers, said to be smugglers', and from yachts,
equally, the way a police cordon holds a mob
from criminals or from celebrities—celebrities,
who sailed through the graying permanent-waves
and tousles of the crowd, ahead
of the eye of the hurricane and docked quick,
though timbers might be sprung from lunging through breakers
and rot, beneath paint, be as sure as taxes for war.

A man, who dreams storms stilled, a man
who can't keep from picking his nose
but hopes to eventually be worthy of ultimate beauty,
a graying man in a gray canvas chair in a rented garden must try
to plant flowers for others to steal from where
a truth, that was too damned grim for him to take, will lie.

Ascending a Madrone Tree for a View of the Pacific, and Remembering the Columbus Day Storm

Feeling familiar limbs' smooth skin, he sees,
again, the slenderer, then, bole bend, when
a hurricane, named for an earlier invader, slammed
against land and twisted roots into air

still storming from the tongue of a poet he loved
to the verge of suicide, and she abandons him
once more, down there where their feet pressed into grass
their shadows, joined to withstand devastating wind,

while leaves, bark, branches, trees and a day,
which had seemed one in their forever, disappeared.

Love Poem for a Woman Who Is a Complete Stranger

Once last night, after drinks, your eyes,
despite your husband, despite my date— What
did you learn? That I was stronger—or more desperate—
could still—had to still—look love, yearning, hurt
and hate, and not break—or, God help me, melt?

What, today, as you look past
my eyes, not to have to look away, what
do you know that I will not ever know?
What could we have done
with our bodies we washed at the cold tap
and rode as if they were real
and reflected pristine marriage barges of warrior and princess,
to wreck in rapids—from which we have navigated,
it seems, to this civilized shore—what could we have done
worse than what we did last night,
your eyes, gleaming to candles, crude nails
from which our naked bodies hung,
confessions posted on Puritan church doors—
our bodies, then, our parents' parents' fears—or
the ragged laundry we'd see Sundays dangling from
glistening thorns, the last smut put
to the inquisition of the Spanish sun.

This morning, your body, and eyes—
your arrogant, frightened, suffering
and questioning eyes—are your own, your own
and mine, and beautiful, beautiful still.

Sunrise Incident on Train, Starting to Start Over

Dawn's glaciers blushing, a woman, distressed
that she's only dressed
in underpants, bra and a ring, smiles

when a stranger smiles that he knows her
intent isn't to dislodge his poem poised,
like eternity's blizzards' avalanche in his brain.

Her beauty, mirrored on breath-clouded window, backed
by a shadowed plunge—and that the two of them could
create a moment, a life, a future beyond
their own—moves him
nearer his reflection's tactful expression of
awareness that her urgent need has more
to do with human digestion than with love.

Unavoidably touching his lonely body briefly, she
hurries down the narrow corridor and disappears,
decorously, behind a door, while steel wheels bear
him over snow
he once was lost in,
horizon's train-tracks' convergence and lines
on a page: signs that he may
have survived.

Storm, Atlantic and Pacific

Hem seething sea foam, wind
a demon hand
ripping white clothing from
decorum—

daphne, perhaps,
beneath tumultuous drifts
and sky, as daunting as
what's fallen from it—

a man sees a woman, young, then,
her skirt surf furled, as pale
as the sail of a vessel about
some sense of herself he may not ever—

no more than a navigator,
at anchor in harbor, can—

even begin
to partly understand.

VI. An History of Some Struggles Against Extinction

The Beautiful Silver

Your hand around a pen, think
of the hands it has held,
whole human beings
hinted by pressure of fingers.

"It's destiny," you write, or "Hell,
it wouldn't've worked,"

words colder than Shakespeare's pages' snow
crammed between collar and giggle, all
of your lovers in mirrors, preparing for meetings,

those futures the beautiful silver
of shattering glass.

To Win Love

after the Sacred Formulas of the Yunwiya

*for John and Mary Ax, husband and wife and Yunwiya
(Cherokee) Medicine Man and Woman*

Finding, emblazoned in your mind,
stud horse, buck deer, buck elk,
warnings of others' intentions of possession,

say: to the woman you love,

"Spring dawn,"

words to help wind
stir ashes of earth, newly begun,
to erupt into life.

"Spring dawn,"

in petals only nostrils can fondle,
your pain the music of harsh rain
gentled by leaves
returned, from the anguish of winter, in buds.

"Spring dawn."

Children's children's children's descendants'
memorial-mounds'
and the highest peaks'
snows, become rain,
and sustain, again, and again,
bright floral decorations, for
funereal occasions, or for, for all
who live, a wedding celebration,
yours.

Snowbound in Deep Woods

for Ingrid

This was my idea: to sew
two pieces of toast
loosely together and throw
them over the cabin roof,

to catch on branches
instead of sinking in snow
too deep for bird beaks
or for us to wade,

and, then, each with the same idea,
we wove our bodies together,

a forest of blizzard all around,

neither we nor the birds knowing if
the two slices of bread
were all we had.

Knitting Needles Warm

for Ingrid and for my father's mother, Mary Turner Salisbury

For fun, my drunken soldier uncle's bullets drove nails,
deep into house
and out, light-beam's gleams
Grandmother's needles, which knitted warmth for one
of her grandsons,
soon gone to do some darning of his own, his plane
drawing white yarn through blue,
weaving through the heavens such legends as
Democracy and Liberty,
which fray more, war after war.

From parents' parents' parents' arms,
which worms turned to skeins
unraveling to cover volcanoes' old age, God could,
with my wife's and my bodies, knit someone new.

Here lie—though bombers still stain sky—
two knitting needles warm
from hands I pray
may ply their simple skills until
the Judgement Day.

For Martina Erin Marie, My Newborn Daughter

Erin to men on the moon   the Big Sandy Valley   that grew
my dad   is tinier than your grin   less   to astronauts
careless technicians launched after our Cherokee ancestors
Spaniards caught and after Christians   dipped in wax
and ignited   to light Roman Legions home

A boy buried under my hair   grown gray as smoke   wants
to give you his midnight arrowhead   its strata of sunset
"blood"   to entertain "Baby"   a soldier now   while Mom
beat diapers white on rocks   Mom   for whose homeland you
Erin   were named   and you were born because I saw my own
tombstone   as lava   ablaze in loving eyes.

Driving from My Daughter's Birth

for Martina

My autumn breath on glass
a membrane taut
near birth,

cars vivid as flecks of blood
beyond this hospital,

my daughter's small fist curls
around a steering-wheel
to meet a future father
driving—too fast,
too fast—to meet a future mother.

Girl Passing House Where I Live with Wife and Baby Daughter

something about
      the rain stains on her backpack
the weary set
      of legs tanned
to the edges of white shorts
      and her head's lift   gives
the boy who ambles   half stoned   down off
      his porch across the street
to kiss her dry mouth   more than
      he'll get

Aeons of Wishes

The plum tree scratching hundreds of matches against
a sky as black as the ceiling I'll stare at
more centuries than I can say, my mother comes,
summoned to cries of children frightened by lightning,

as her mother came,
not screaming from cancer gnawing intestines but calm
and giving me cookies, a substitute grandma the one
resurrection my Christian mom could offer her "Wild
Indian" son, who was four
and bored by all the lovey talk and strangers' names
and finally stole some matches, which,
when hit with rocks, cracked like cap-pistol shots—

Dad drunk and shooting at ghosts again
myself my mother's "little man"
begging him to behave.

He grew quiet, then
quieter still,
too quiet now for his kid,
whose days of naughtiness—or most
or some—have gone
into wish for understanding.

The pear belongs to the grandmother next door,
who lit—years freeing her
from city safety-laws—Mexican rockets,
last Fourth of July, liberating sky
over Monroe Street, Madison, Jefferson and

Friendly, my daughter's president.

She's five this fall,
her birthday candle flames

leaves of the plum,
aeons of wishes starring a black cloud sky.

New Oil into Old Leather

The gray of muddy fields,
which fed to womanhood
your bride, these are the boots you wore
when you were courting her,
so long ago she has become
as mysterious as her ancestors,
in moccasins, before your
progenitors invaded.

With maybe years of wear
still in good leather, you rub,
until sun dawns in shine,
and you walk again, to a home
so beautiful you may be
forever in learning to sing its name.

A Widower, the Old Geologist Tries Not to Awake

Asleep, he is young, bride
matching his stride through the must
of winters past,
her nostrils flared for spring.

Tip of the topmost leaf becomes,
in first faint dawn, the deepest root-thrust
seeking Earth's core's hidden sun, and he

soars through shake-shingles, a man with his mate—
two stones exploded from everything else, not doomed
to orbit eternally
a dead star's dark world,
but to circle children's children's children's
lava-dust flower-beds,

giving direction, brightening sky.

Sunset and Lilacs

Only orchards' roots feeding on fruit,
"Feel heavy," he'd say,
"as if, one spoonful more, and, floor
splintering under armpits, I'd
dangle into cellar, where rats
could gnash at toenails till
they'd worn fangs down to gums,

"but if the missus would slip through our door,
sunset and blossoms around her, to catch
me dreaming, her chair's rusted springs
would trill like robins, glad—
as I rose, lightened of these words—

that their own slender owner'd returned."

History or Some

While TV nations, as is usual,
fumble momentous decisions,
my wife and I are in a kitchen we
no longer own and maybe never did.

The oat bran I ate, to encourage my damaged heart
is now air, shelved in rectangular air,
whose door might prefer to be
poeticized as the ghost of a tree.

But—despite history's unimaginative recipes
for meat—the cry of the cat,
which shared, for night after night
of its life, with book after book, my lap,
cries from the dark,

in which I wake and think,
that sounds like my child,
who needs me, or,
years gone, it may be some other I hear.

Veterans Day, 2002, Politicians Threatening War

Words to be bombs,
exploded into streets,
staining survivors' fleeing feet red, our hearts play
piano on our ribs—improvisation, a kitten's stumbling steps,
its claws drawn in, in fear of the unfamiliar—

hard lessons our
and our enemies' children
have got to learn.

VII. A Vanishing American's Struggle Against Vanishing

A Ritual to Not Feel Alone

These are wild swans, that fly
reflected clouds
in those soon to evaporate ponds,
our aging eyes.

Though born of natural birds,
these are the air
of words, in our minds,
in the only moment you
and I, strangers to one another,
are apt to share; and sun—
which vision and life depend upon—fledged wings
from actual migrations of rain's
and wind's white foam.

Our swans—gobbling sedge
and gabbling swans' love
of swans and of being swans—
and we, strangers no longer, may
for a time, stay
in somebody's ears, eyes, brain,
when all that we know
as real has gone,
for good—or has merely migrated,
we could just as certainly say.

For My Swinomish Brother Drumming Across the Water

I am an old one, not selling what will sell
along the road to what has already been sold.

I am both brother and killer of Deer, whose hide
I strip from meat my family must eat or starve,
and I offer the remainder back to our common home,
having lived so many seasons of venison I feel
it is Deer who plucks blossoms from pastures I'd share
forever, or as far as air has anything to give to sky.

Sleep Chant

for Joe Bruchac

Yay o,

like cells I was made from,

my thoughts become salmon
swimming as one,

braving dark breakers inside my head,

battling the current
   which batters flesh against stone

and reaching the stream they were spawned in

and hands,
   which held hands,
   made fists,
   squeezed trigger,
   moved pen,

subside,

this poem a tidepool

emptied of all
save sky.

Age 77, I Climb to Indian Ridge's Fire-Lookout Tower and Search for Lineage

Gestated from sand and fires
as fierce as those mating smoke
with clouds near here, glass walls,
although as clear as poets or parents alert
for danger, seem siblings of old volcanoes' stone.

Ink an eruption, of dew-drop dimension, I find
a closer kinship with the wooden tower's chronology's
sagas of growth-rings, still being written by cones
below this peak, but, generations of giant pines
charred to the roots, living flesh cooked to the hoofs
or claws in my brain, and any human's life
possibly only this moment, between hate
and other mistakes and love and eternity,
my family's history to date's final dot's a bee,
as black as a cindered earth, orbiting sun
in a crimson blossom, doomed
but yet a promise of centuries
of beauty for grandchildren soon to be born.

After Heart Surgery

My wishbone split
then wired back together, I wish
to go on baring my heart
for the yet to be born
and am visited by Sir Walter Raleigh,
whose breast could have been halved—
his intestines put to flames—
his testicles cut—but that
his sentence was lightened to
lopping his love-poem-crammed head.

My Cherokee dad sang my Irish mom
an English courting song,
with no apparent anger about
invasion, torture and massacre—his peace pipe filled
with Sir Walter Raleigh pipe tobacco, until he
suffered the fate postponed for me.

The need to share irony—
which helps one endure pain—past,

two visitors leave by, but leave ajar, a door
not even doctors can bear to know is there.

After Heart-Bypass Surgery, Another Ritual for Continuing Struggle

To save my heart, veins,
from legs which paraded through World War Two, have,
like loyal royal guards, been sent to higher ground,
delaying overthrow,

but two big dogs, teeth sharper than pen, intend to end
my history, the foot trying to defend
weakened, from redeployment of blood, and shod with soft
rubber—from trees French Legionnaires ordered planted
by Indo-Chinese, tapped now by Vietnamese,
supplying an American corporation named, for victory, Nike.

Heedlessly—or, as historians say of our country—
"terribly" young, the dogs' companions demand
reassurance that lack of licenses, leashes and
rabies-inoculations won't end
their best friends' freedom.

Never, in my grim time, so young,
I place my plight with that
of buffalo hunted, not for food but for fun,
to near extinction and with that
of my Cherokee forebears,

and keep carefully quiet, until,
again beyond the reach of jaws
stronger than mine, I seize,
between worn, grave-spade-shape
Vanishing American incisors,
my right to whine, to growl, to warn, to bite and to
the next breath.

Caring for the Soon to be Born

This, for all I can know, my last breath
of our ever more poisonous atmosphere,
to be shaped into word or not,
I hear bulls' bellowing survival intentions,
and write that my father wrote,
on the walls of our barn, the times
of colossal matings and the times
when calves would have to be—
following centuries of bovine captivity,
for humans' prolonged nursing—tugged free
from exhausted cows and rubbed dry and warm,
with "gunny-sacks,"
named for the ones bulged by powder for cannon to kill
millions of my Native American people.

Emerging, paired, as if in prayer,
to be grasped by helpful hands, small hoofs,
glistening like seashells,
made deep prints in my brain,
which puberty had turned into Science class's primal-mud,

and, now, a final heartbeat likely to leave
grandchildren and poems not yet formed,
I write that: stub-pencil sharpened on trigger-finger nail,
Dad scribbled as devotedly as he had strummed
the strings of his banjo, for crowd after crowd,
and, then, for my mom
and for five children, until
applause, stampeding hoofs or cannonade
stilled in his chest, he left me,
to scribble the times
of destinies, which would—
war not yet nuclear—be born.

A Prophecy, Wish, Hope or Prayer

Old World, whose curled longitudes I know,
as I knew toes,
crammed
to help gums endure the first
eruptions since birth, I've learned

some metaphors of lips
and nipples and beds'
seasons of plowing, planting and cultivating, and,

more fragile than eyelids,
petals still open on dawn,

while wind's diurnal doggerel's theme remains the same
as perennial poems' usual impossible:

"She loves me not, she—"
our Mother-Earth-Lover-Earth—"loves me,"

an answer for all who need more than
eternity's uncertainty,

syllables crammed
to ease skull's
unbearably perishable brain.

Ralph Salisbury, Professor Emeritus of the University of Oregon, is the author of two books of short fiction and seven books of poetry, the most recent of which, *Rainbows of Stone* (University of Arizona Press), was chosen by Maxine Kumin as a finalist in the Oregon Book Awards. Other poetry titles include *A White Rainbow, Poems of a Cherokee Heritage*; *Going to the Water; Spirit Beast Chant; Pointing at the Rainbow; Ghost Grapefruit and Other Poems;* and *Poesie Da Un Retaggio Cherokee* (Multimedia Edizioni, Salerno, Italy). His short fiction titles include *One Indian and Two Chiefs* (Navajo C. College Press) and *The Last Rattlesnake Throw* (University of Oklahoma Press).

Printed in the United States
68643LVS00002B/31-39